Introductory Course

TEACHER'S NOTES and ANSWER KEY
Developmental Language and Sentence Skills Guided Practice
Support for *Warriner's Handbook*

- **Grammar**
- **Usage**
- **Mechanics**
- **Sentences**

HOLT, RINEHART AND WINSTON

Copyright © by Holt, Rinehart and Winston

All rights reserved. No part of this publication may be reproduced or transmitted in any form or by any means, electronic or mechanical, including photocopy, recording, or any information storage and retrieval system, without permission in writing from the publisher.

Teachers using HOLT TRADITIONS may photocopy blackline masters in complete pages in sufficient quantities for classroom use only and not for resale.

HOLT, HRW, and the **"Owl Design"** are trademarks licensed to Holt, Rinehart and Winston, registered in the United States of America and/or other jurisdictions.

Printed in the United States of America

If you have received these materials as examination copies free of charge, Holt, Rinehart and Winston retains title to the materials and they may not be resold. Resale of examination copies is strictly prohibited.

Possession of this publication in print format does not entitle users to convert this publication, or any portion of it, into electronic format.

ISBN 978-0-55-400187-6
ISBN 0-55-400187-X

8 9 10 11   1186   21 20 19 18
4500707330

Contents

To the Teacher v
Summary of Parts of Speech xiii
Summary of Parts of a Sentence xiv
Summary of Subject-Verb Agreement xv
Summary of Uses of the Comma xvi

Chapter 1
THE PARTS OF A SENTENCE

Sentences and Sentence Fragments 1
The Subject 1
The Predicate 1

Chapter 2
**PARTS OF SPEECH OVERVIEW:
NOUN, PRONOUN, ADJECTIVE**

The Noun 3
Personal, Reflexive, and Intensive Pronouns 3
Demonstrative and Relative Pronouns 4
Indefinite and Interrogative Pronouns 4
The Adjective 4

Chapter 3
**PARTS OF SPEECH OVERVIEW:
VERB, ADVERB, PREPOSITION, CONJUNCTION,
INTERJECTION**

The Verb 5
Action Verbs and Linking Verbs 5
The Adverb 5
The Preposition 6
The Conjunction and the Interjection 6

Chapter 4
**THE PHRASE AND THE CLAUSE:
PREPOSITIONAL PHRASES, INDEPENDENT AND
SUBORDINATE CLAUSES, SENTENCE STRUCTURE**

The Prepositional Phrase 7
The Adjective Phrase 7
The Adverb Phrase 8
The Clause 8
The Adjective Clause 8
The Adverb Clause 9
Simple Sentences and Compound Sentences 9
Complex Sentences and
    Compound-Complex Sentences 10

Chapter 5
**COMPLEMENTS:
DIRECT AND INDIRECT OBJECTS,
SUBJECT COMPLEMENTS**

Direct Objects and Indirect Objects 11
Predicate Nominatives and
    Predicate Adjectives 11

Chapter 6
**AGREEMENT:
SUBJECT AND VERB, PRONOUN AND ANTECEDENT**

Subject-Verb Agreement 12
Subject-Verb Agreement: Indefinite Pronouns 12
Subject-Verb Agreement: Compound Subjects 12
Pronoun-Antecedent Agreement A 12
Pronoun-Antecedent Agreement B 13

Chapter 7
**USING VERBS CORRECTLY:
PRINCIPAL PARTS, REGULAR AND
IRREGULAR VERBS, TENSE**

Principal Parts of Verbs 14
Regular Verbs 14
Irregular Verbs A 14
Irregular Verbs B 14
Irregular Verbs C 15
Verb Tense 15
Sit and *Set*, *Rise* and *Raise*, *Lie* and *Lay* A 15
Sit and *Set*, *Rise* and *Raise*, *Lie* and *Lay* B 16

Chapter 8
**USING PRONOUNS CORRECTLY:
SUBJECT AND OBJECT FORMS**

The Forms of Personal Pronouns 17
The Subject Form 17
The Object Form 17
Special Pronoun Problems 17

Contents

Chapter 9
**USING MODIFIERS CORRECTLY:
COMPARISON AND PLACEMENT**

Forms of Modifiers **19**
Degrees of Comparison **19**
Regular and Irregular Comparison **19**
Special Problems in Using Modifiers **19**
Placement of Modifiers....................................**20**

Chapter 10
**A GLOSSARY OF USAGE:
COMMON USAGE PROBLEMS**

Glossary of Usage A **21**
Glossary of Usage B **21**

Chapter 11
**CAPITAL LETTERS:
RULES FOR CAPITALIZATION**

First Words; Letter Salutations and Closings;
    The Pronoun *I* **22**
Proper Nouns A **22**
Proper Nouns B **22**
Proper Nouns C **23**
Titles of Creative Works **24**

Chapter 12
**PUNCTUATION:
END MARKS, SEMICOLONS, COLONS, AND COMMAS**

Commas...**25**
Commas and Semicolons with
    Compound Sentences **25**
Colons **25**

Chapter 13
**PUNCTUATION:
UNDERLINING (ITALICS), QUOTATION MARKS, APOSTROPHES**

Underlining (Italics) and
    Quotation Marks with Titles **27**
Quotation Marks **27**
Apostrophes **27**
Parentheses **28**

Chapter 14
**SPELLING:
IMPROVING YOUR SPELLING**

Words with *ie* and *ei* **29**
Prefixes and Suffixes **29**
Plurals of Nouns **29**
Words Often Confused A **29**
Words Often Confused B **30**
Words Often Confused C **30**

Chapter 15
**CORRECTING COMMON ERRORS:
KEY LANGUAGE SKILLS REVIEW**

Common Errors Review..................................**31**

Chapter 16
WRITING EFFECTIVE SENTENCES

Complete Sentences and Sentence Fragments..........**32**
Run-on Sentences...**32**
Combining Sentences by Inserting Words **32**
Combining Sentences by Inserting
    Groups of Words...**32**
Combining Sentences by Using Connecting
    Words; Joining Subjects and Verbs **33**

To the Teacher

The worksheets in the student edition are designed for students who should be capable of doing on-grade level English work, but who, for whatever reason, have encountered a grammatical skill or concept that they are having difficulty mastering. You can now intervene by selecting practice exercises designed to help the student master that specific grammatical skill or concept. You can then give the selected worksheets to that student as an extra assignment that complements ongoing class work. Of course, it is important that the student with the deficiency also continue to participate in the regular class work so that he or she does not fall further behind. Worksheets can be used as daily or weekly take-home assignments, or they can be completed during times of the day designated for personal study. Occasionally, a student's grammatical misunderstanding might be so specific that the problem could be solved in one worksheet assignment. Often, however, the worksheet assignments will be more extensive. In fact, some students may rely on the worksheets for continual support throughout the school year.

The worksheets can also be used in conjunction with composition instruction. When a student writes an essay that contains one-too-many errors in the possessive case, for example, you can merely staple a possessive case worksheet to the student's paper to be completed along with the essay corrections. This method allows you to individualize grammatical instruction while you continue discussing the principles of composition with the whole class. It also allows you to help your students see the interdependency of the study of composition and the study of grammar.

Beyond the immediate benefits to your lessons in grammar and in composition, the worksheets can help with the long-term goal of boosting scores on state-mandated tests. In this regard, you will likely discover that even strong students have an Achilles' heel. For these students you can select practice worksheets that will target a particular weakness.

Finally, after a student has completed the selected worksheet assignments and you are fairly confident that he or she has mastered the point of grammar (say, direct objects), it is important to acknowledge the accomplishment publicly. For example, you may be teaching a lesson on adjective clauses. During your discussion, you could call on a student who has mastered direct objects, "Edward, does this adjective clause have a direct object?" Edward gets to demonstrate his new expertise in front of his peers and can feel that he is no longer somehow separated from the mainstream of his classmates. This method will also associate the worksheets in the minds of the students with something positive, rather than with a notion of punishment.

Although the concepts in the following worksheets are presented in a very basic and concrete way, students who are struggling may benefit from an additional step in the teaching process. I have found that when my students and I use a consistent pattern of questions and responses in our discussions of grammar, learning becomes easier. I have incorporated many of these patterns in the sections that follow.

In the following tips to the teacher, you will also notice that I have consistently used one line under the subject, two lines under the verb, parentheses around prepositional phrases, and arrows from all modifiers to the words they modify. I have found that this consistent systematic approach has worked especially well for students who

- have attention-deficit disorder,
- find logical reasoning difficult,
- are generally disorganized,
- find grammar too abstract to remember on a long-term or even a short-term basis.

The use of symbols (underlining, parentheses, and arrows) provides a visual cue that students can use to identify what they already know so that they then can more easily focus on what they don't know.

THE SENTENCE

When I started teaching grammar many years ago, I tended to downplay this topic, thinking that just about everybody knew what a sentence was and could easily identify the subject and the verb. I was so eager to get on to the more sophisticated aspects of grammar that I failed to lay the proper foundation and, consequently, caused unnecessary confusion in my students.

Many of your students may know a sentence when they see one but may be unfamiliar with the vocabulary used to discuss sentences. Familiarizing students with the terms *subject*, *predicate*, and *verb* is essential since these are terms that will be used throughout their study of grammar.

The Subject

I tell students that the **subject** of a sentence is who or what the sentence is talking about. I write a sentence on the board and then ask, "Who or what is this sentence about?" When someone answers correctly, I underline the entire subject with one line, emphasizing the consistent use of this marking system. If the student leaves out part of the subject, I remind him or her to include the subject's modifiers. Next, I ask, "Can anyone show me the main word in the subject, the one that, more than any other word, tells what the sentence is about?" When a student comes up with the answer, I write "*ss*" over the simple subject. So far, the sentence might look like this:

The old *ss* road along the coast leads you to the beach.

The Predicate

I explain that a **predicate** is everything that is said about the subject. Continuing with the previous sentence, I ask the class, "What is everything that the sentence says about *the old road along the coast*?" When a student answers correctly, I double underline "leads you to the beach." Then, I explain that, in the predicate, the main word is the **verb**, which tells most about what the subject is doing or is being. When a student locates the verb *leads*, I write *v* over it. On the board, I vary the sentence to look like this:

The old road along the coast *v* is the best way to the beach.

I explain that here the road is not doing anything; the verb *is* just indicates existence.

Next, we turn to **helping (auxiliary) verbs.** I explain that helping verbs can be used with both action and linking verbs, and I give many examples of both. I have found it extremely useful to supply students with a list of helping verbs to memorize:

- These helping verbs will always have a main verb after them: *shall, should, will, would, may, might, can, could, must, ought.*

- These forms of the verb *to be* can be used as helping verbs as well as linking or state-of-being verbs: *(to) be, am, is, are, was, were, being, been.*

- These forms of the verb *to have* and *to do* can be used as helping verbs as well as action verbs: *have, has, had* and *do, does, did.*

To help students find the subject and the verb, I first stress the importance of understanding what the sentence is saying. Students who are having trouble with this assignment should read each sentence three times before they begin. Second, I ask them to find the verb and underline it twice, not leaving out any part of it. Third, we ask the subject question (who or what did that [or is that]?) and we draw one line under the answer to that question. It is important to include in the examples some imperative sentences, so that students can work with the understood "you."

Remind students to be on the lookout for interrogative sentences. These sentences often begin with a helping verb, followed by the subject, and then the main verb. For example, "Do you like pasta?" Also, encourage students to say "subject of the verb" instead of "subject of the sentence" or just "subject." This repetition reinforces the students' understanding of the function of the subject.

If your students have studied prepositional phrases, remind them that the object of a preposition can never be the simple subject. Encourage students to "corral" these phrases by putting parentheses around them. Setting them off from the rest of the sentence at this point helps the students focus more clearly on the simple subject and verb.

PARTS OF SPEECH

Learning the eight parts of speech is important for students because, with this vocabulary, a discussion of other grammatical concepts becomes more productive. However, students must understand that a word's part of speech is usually not rigidly fixed. I show students that the same word can be a different part of speech in a different sentence. The word *down* demonstrates this idea particularly well since it can function as five of the eight parts of speech.

Nouns

Tell students that they can easily remember what a noun is because it begins with the letter *n* and so does the word *name*. A noun names something. A noun is anything you can talk about, including things you can't see, such as love, power, and happiness. Tell students that if they're not sure that a word is a noun in a particular sentence, to put *a* or *the* in front of the word, and if *a* or *the* makes sense, the word is probably a noun.

Pronouns

I motivate students to think about pronouns by pointing out that we use pronouns without even thinking about them. When I give them the sentence "I bought a pizza; the pizza had mushrooms on the pizza," they can immediately see the usefulness of pronouns. We intuitively prefer "I bought a pizza; it had mushrooms on it." I show students that they already know how to use pronouns, although they may not understand what a pronoun is: It takes the place of a noun.

Adjectives

Ask students to close their eyes and to picture a pile of books. Then, tell students that each of them probably has completely different books pictured in his or her mind, yet all of them are imagining books. Tell the students they are going to modify, or change, the image they have by adding adjectives to their *books*. Then say, "thick books." Then, "thick, green books." Then, "thick, green, leather books." Then, "These four thick, green, leather books." All these adjectives have made the noun *books* more specific, by answering the questions *Which? What kind of?* and *How many?* Be sure not to omit the last example using a number because students may overlook the fact that numbers can be adjectives.

I encourage my students to draw an arrow from the adjective to the noun or pronoun it modifies. To reinforce the meaning of this visual, I tell students that an adjective is like a dog on a leash; it stays close to its master, the noun or pronoun it is describing. Remind students that adjectives are usually right in front of the nouns or pronouns they modify but that they can also follow linking verbs as predicate adjectives.

When you ask a student to tell you why a word is an adjective, encourage this pattern of response: "Because it's not just any old book, it's a green book." "Because it's not just any old dog, it's a shaggy dog." "Because it's not just any old shoe, it's a dirty shoe," and so forth. The repetition of this pattern, however absurd it sounds, effectively instills in the student's mind an understanding of how adjectives function.

Adverbs

Adverbs seem to be the hardest part of speech for students to master. I ask students to be patient. Sometimes learning something worthwhile takes a little time.

After defining the term and giving a few examples of typical adverbs ending in *–ly*, I explain further that an adverb could be any word that answers the question *How? When?* or *Where?* Continually stress these basic adverb questions. When you ask students why a particular word is an adverb, encourage them to begin their response with the words *because it tells* and then to choose from the questions *How? When?* or *Where?* to complete their answer.

I rarely go to the movies.

Rarely do I go to the movies.

I go to the movies rarely.

I encourage my students to draw an arrow to the verb, adjective, or other adverb that the adverb is modifying.

You can use a pair of sentences, such as the following, to model the distinction between adjectives and adverbs:

She is a *fast* runner.

She runs *fast*.

In both sentences, ask students: Does *fast* answer any of the adjective questions: *Which one? What kind? How many?* Or does it answer any of the adverb questions: *How? When? Where?* Encourage students to draw arrows from *fast* to the word it modifies in each sentence.

Prepositions

First, have students memorize a short list of common prepositions, such as *at, in, on, by, for, from, near,* and *with*. Learning this short list enables students to set up a mental paradigm, which helps them identify new prepositions. Then explain that a preposition shows a relationship between its object and another word in the sentence. Have students hold a pencil in their hand. Then say, while you are doing the same thing with your pencil, "Place the pencil **on** your desk, now, **beside** the desk, **under** the desk, **against** the desk, **above** the desk; move the pencil **around** the desk." This kind of physical involvement helps the student understand what a preposition does.

Conjunctions

The lesson on coordinating conjunctions seems to be an easy one for most students. (We will save the more difficult subordinate conjunctions for the lesson on adverb clauses.) I usually just remind students to be on the lookout for conjunctions when identifying subjects, verbs and prepositional phrases. A student who does not read a sentence carefully might be inclined to pick out just half of a compound subject, verb, or object of a preposition.

Interjections

Since interjections are not grammatically connected to the rest of the sentence, they are the easiest part of speech for students to recognize. You may want to have your students memorize the short list of interjections given in the textbook.

COMPLEMENTS

Explain that not all sentences will contain a complement. Some sentences don't need one. Some do. *I sneezed* makes sense all by itself, but *I hit* cries out for another word to answer *What? Whom?* Tell students that this word that completes the meaning of the verb is a complement. It looks like the word *complete*, and that's exactly what a complement does: It completes the meaning of the verb.

Remind students that they can help themselves recognize complements by underlining the subject once and the verb twice and by crossing out prepositional phrases.

PHRASES

I explain that a phrase is a group of words used as a single part of speech.

Prepositional Phrases

Review with students the list of common prepositions. Also, remind them that a preposition shows a relationship between its object and some other word in the sentence. Show students how an object of a preposition answers the question *What?* or *Whom?* when we ask the question in this way: First, say the preposition; then, ask *What?* or *Whom?* On the board, for example, write, "The pencil is on the desk." Then ask, "On what?" Give the answer, "The desk. *Desk* is the object of the preposition." Then, note that the answer to the question, the object, is a noun or a pronoun. Put numerous examples on the board, and in a relaxed atmosphere, check for understanding by calling on individuals to ask and answer the object-of-the-preposition question. Point out that a prepositional phrase begins with a preposition and ends with a noun or pronoun. It includes any modifiers that come between these two parts of speech.

Encourage students to place parentheses around all prepositional phrases. Parentheses here, as in math, indicate that the material within them functions as a single unit. The prepositional phrase (in parentheses) will work as an adjective unit or an adverb unit. I have found that "corralling" prepositional phrases into parentheses greatly facilitates teaching subject-verb agreement and helps to keep students focused on the basic structure of a sentence. Many students over the years have told me that this practice has been useful in helping them to read and understand other school subjects.

After students put parentheses around a prepositional phrase, ask them to draw an arrow from the phrase to the word it modifies. Using pairs of sentences such as the following helps students see the relationship between simple adjectives and adjective phrases.

The *corner* house is hers. [Adjective]

The house (*on the corner*) is hers. [Prepositional phrase used as an adjective]

In the same way, students can learn to see the relationship between adverbs and adverb phrases.

She walked *home*. [Adverb]

She walked (*to her house*.) [Prepositional phrase used as an adverb]

Participial Phrases

Tell students that a participial phrase is a group of words that is used as an adjective. The main word in a participial phrase is the present or past participle form of a verb. To help students identify present and past participles, tell them to look for verb forms that end in *ing*, or *ed*, *n*, or *en*. Then, have students check to be sure the verb form is used as an adjective and not as a noun.

Present Participial Phrases

To help students distinguish between participles used as verbs and participles used as adjectives, use a series of three sentences such as the following.

The frog is **jumping** on the lily pads. [verb]

The **jumping** frog landed in the water. [participle] [Point out to students that it's not just any old frog that landed in the water; it's the jumping frog.]

The frog, **jumping on the lily pads,** landed in the water. [present participial phrase, made up of the participle plus a modifying prepositional phrase] [Point out to students again the adjective function of the participial phrase. It's not just any old frog; it's the frog *jumping on the lily pads.*]

You may want to point out at this time that verb forms ending in *ing* can also work as nouns. These nouns are called gerunds, and students will learn about them at another time. Just provide a brief example: *Learning about gerunds* is fun! In this sentence the gerund phrase *Learning about gerunds* is a noun phrase, subject of the verb *is. What* is fun? Learning about gerunds.

Past Participial Phrases

Similarly, we can use a series of three sentences to distinguish past participles used as modifiers from past participles used as verbs.

The branches were **broken** by the wind. (verb)

The **broken** branches lay on the ground. (adjective) [Point out that not just any old branches lay on the ground; they were the *broken* branches.]

The branches, **broken by the wind,** lay on the ground. (past participial phrase) [Point out again that it's not any old branches; it's just the ones that were broken by the wind.]

Infinitive Phrases

When teaching infinitives, I remind the students that one of the characteristics of verbs is tense, or time. Unlike a finite, conjugated verb, an infinitive has no time constraints binding it: It is infinite.

ix

After explaining that an infinitive can function as an adjective, adverb, or noun, stress that students can determine how an infinitive is used by asking:

- Does this infinitive answer the adjective questions?
- Does it answer the adverb questions?
- Does it function as a noun, in one of the noun positions in the sentence?

Appositive Phrases

To help your students remember the purpose of an appositive, you can put an equals sign above the first comma in the phrase to reinforce that the phrase equals or means the same thing as the noun or pronoun before it:

=
Mr. Jones, **my brother's teacher,** is going to Spain.

I remind students to think of the commas that come before and after nonessential appositive phrases as handles. They can hold on to both handles and lift the phrase right out of the sentence. A nonessential phrase is an interrupter; it doesn't really need to be there.

CLAUSES

An effective mnemonic device for teaching clauses is a picture of an eagle with its claws outstretched. In one claw it clutches a placard with the word "subject" and in the other claw, a placard with the word "verb." The eagle swoops down on a sentence and grabs the subject with one claw and the verb with the other. Now it has a CLAUSE in its CLAWS! Use the fingers of both hands to make claws that "grab" on to a subject **and** a verb every time the class analyzes a clause. My students never seem to forget this image.

Adjective Clauses

Adjective clauses are fairly easy for students to identify because most begin with relative pronouns. Encourage students to memorize these identifiers. You might want to explain that "relative" refers to how this pronoun relates back to a noun or pronoun in another clause and, thus, ties the adjective clause into that clause.

Be sure that students see the relationship between adjectives and adjective clauses. Use a pair of sentences such as the following to demonstrate the connection.

Our **Florida** relatives are visiting us. [adjective]

Our relatives **who live in Florida** are visiting us. [adjective clause]

To reinforce the concept that an adjective clause functions as a modifier, encourage students to draw an arrow from the adjective clause to the noun or pronoun it is modifying.

Adverb Clauses

Adverb clauses begin with words called subordinating conjunctions. Tell your students that if they memorize a list of common subordinating conjunctions, it will be easy for them to identify adverb clauses. Warn students that several subordinating conjunctions can also be used as prepositions or as adverbs. Therefore, if there is no subject and verb after the subordinating conjunction, there is no clause, and what we thought was a subordinating conjunction is actually a preposition or an adverb.

Have you eaten tofu **before?** [adverb]

We had supper **before the game.** [preposition]

Before we ordered, we asked for some water. [adverb clause]

Using the three sentences above, point out to students the relationship of the adverb clause to the adverb and the adverb phrase. Encourage students to draw an arrow from the adverb clause to the verb, adjective, or other adverb it is modifying.

Once they learn about adverb clauses, I encourage my students to use them often in their writing, especially introductory adverb clauses. These clauses pique the curiosity of the reader and, consequently, make the students' writing more interesting: Starting a sentence with *When they found a small key* makes the reader curious about what might happen next.

AGREEMENT OF SUBJECT AND VERB

This topic is often difficult for students because the idea of singular and plural verb forms is somewhat meaningless to them. It is important to explain that verbs aren't actually singular and plural, but they take a form that goes with a singular or plural subject.

I have found that the following method invariably works if you are consistent in having students do all the steps.

1. Cross out prepositional phrases that come between the subject and the verb:

    One ~~(of the pages)~~ *was* missing.

2. When the simple subject is singular, whether it is a noun or a pronoun, substitute *he, she,* or *it* (any one of the three will work).

    (She)
    The girl ~~(with the books)~~ *is* my sister.

3. When the subject is plural, substitute *they*.

    (They)
    The reasons ~~(for his success)~~ *are* easy to see.

4. When the following singular indefinite pronouns are subjects, focus on the singular endings *one* or *body*: *one, everyone, everybody, no one, nobody, anyone, someone, somebody.*

5. When the pronouns *each, either,* or *neither* are subjects, think *each one, either one, neither one.*

    (Each one)
    Each ~~(of the students)~~ *has arrived*.

6. Compound subjects connected by *and* take a plural verb form. Substitute the pronoun *they* for subjects joined by *and*.

    (They)
    The coach and his assistant *attend* every game.

7. For subjects connected by *or* or *nor,* look at the subject closest to the verb. If the subject is singular, substitute *he, she,* or *it*. If the subject is plural, substitute *they*. To make the process even easier, just cross out the other subject(s) and the *or* or *nor*.

    (She)
    ~~The twins or~~ my sister *has* my book.

    (They)
    ~~My sister or~~ the twins *have* my book.

8. *Here, there,* and *where* are almost never subjects. If a sentence begins with one of these words, look for the subject after the verb.

    (They)
    There *are* five women on the committee.

9. If the pronoun *you* is the subject, remember that *you* always takes a plural verb form, even when it refers to one person.

MECHANICS

The rules of mechanics, grammar, and usage are interdependent. Therefore, it is sometimes difficult to come up with mechanics tips or tricks that don't require prior knowledge of grammar and usage. Telling students to use a comma between independent clauses joined by a conjunction always assumes that they can recognize independent clauses and conjunctions. One of the best times to bring up many of the following ideas is during discussion of the associated grammar or usage concept.

Capitalization

Most students have no difficulty recognizing *Jennifer* as a proper noun and *student* as a common noun and are not likely to capitalize such words incorrectly. Some students, though, may have more difficulty applying that principle to inanimate objects. Creating a series of sentences such as the following can help reinforce the concept.

If I had a boat, I would name it _____.

A series of sentences like the one above could also be used as additional practice in using italics and quotation marks with titles. Students may be more engaged in learning to capitalize and punctuate names that they have come up with on their own.

xi

Commas

An earlier tip suggested that students think of the commas that come before and after nonessential appositive phrases as handles that can lift the phrase right out of the sentence. This image of commas as handles works equally well with any other nonessential elements. Write a sentence such as the following on the board, with the nonessential clause written well above the rest of the sentence.

, which had been hopping from branch to branch,

The bird began to build its nest.

Alternatively, write the sentence above on strips of paper, one strip for "The bird," one strip for "**, which had been hopping from branch to branch,**" and one strip for "began to build its nest," and have a student or two students pull the nonessential clause out by the handles (the commas.)

Spelling

Because rules for spelling are so numerous (and exceptions can seem even more numerous), students may get discouraged by seeing every one of their spelling errors marked in red. For students who misspell many words, you might suggest that they use a spellchecking program or keep a dictionary handy. Concentrate classroom instruction on words that a spellchecking program might overlook, such as *there, their,* and *they're*. If students can master such commonly confused words, they may feel better about having to reach for a dictionary to find the plural spelling of *thesaurus*, for example.

CONCLUSION

These worksheets can benefit struggling students by helping teachers intervene before problems become crises. Because they are relatively easy to administer and evaluate, they can benefit overworked teachers. However, this strategy is only one of many that are available to us, such as using sentences from students' favorite books, magazines, or songs to model grammatical structures; playing quiz-show grammar games; singing, chanting, or rapping out grammar rules or lists; and allowing students who have mastered a point of grammar to tutor those who are having difficulty.

In teaching grammar, we should also take some time to consider the image of ourselves that we present to our students. For example, we might encourage our students to see us as a coach who is teaching them to field the grammar issues they encounter in their writing, but we must eschew any kind of image that suggests a dry-as-dust pedant or the grammar police. We can avoid the negative images if we remember what we are, and are not, trying to do. We are not trying to teach our students to be petty about errors, nor are we trying to get them to look down on those who speak nonstandard English. Rather, we seek to empower students by helping them master basic language skills.

Adapted from Sentence Surgery: A Systematic and Graphic Method of Grammar Instruction *by Michèle Beck-von-Peccoz. Copyright © 2000 by Michèle Beck-von-Peccoz. Reprinted by permission of the author.*

On the following pages are quick-reference charts that you may wish to copy and distribute to your students.

SUMMARY OF PARTS OF SPEECH

Part of Speech	Use	Examples
noun	names	**Shane** is playing **soccer** in the **park.**
pronoun	takes the place of a noun	**She herself** said **that all** of **us** have been invited
adjective	modifies a noun or pronoun	**This rare Roman** coin is **valuable.**
verb	shows action or a state of being	Shelby **is** the candidate who **will win.**
adverb	modifies a verb, an adjective, or another adverb	I jogged **nearly** five miles **today** but I think I ran **too fast.**
preposition closed	relates a noun or a pronoun to another word	Some **of** the streets were **on** Friday **because of** flooding.
conjunction	joins words or groups of words	**Either** Brandon **or** I will meet you **and** Darla at the airport **so that** you won't have to take a taxi.
interjection	shows emotion	**Hooray!** We're home! **Well,** we'll see.

SUMMARY OF PARTS OF A SENTENCE

Parts of a Sentence	Questions to Ask	Examples
Subject	Who or what is the sentence about?	After lunch, the **members** of the drama club will be taking group pictures.
Verb	What is the subject doing? or What is the subject's state of being?	The slamming door **startled** the birds in the front yard. **Are** you excited about the recital this evening?
Predicate Nominative	Which word completes the meaning of a linking verb and identifies or refers to the subject?	Joseph Ferdinand is the **chairperson** of the volunteer committee.
Predicate Adjective	Which word completes the meaning of a linking verb and describes the subject?	The dogs were **thirsty** after their daily walk.
Direct Object	Which word completes the meaning of an action verb and answers the question *Whom?* or *What?* after the verb?	The principal gave each new teacher a welcoming **gift.**
Indirect Object	Which word answers the question *to whom?* or *to what?* (or *for whom?* or *for what?*) in sentences with direct objects?	The principal gave each new **teacher** a welcoming gift.

SUMMARY OF SUBJECT-VERB AGREEMENT

A verb agrees with its subject in number.

    (1) Singular subjects take singular verbs.   (The **cat sleeps**.)

    (2) Plural subjects take plural verbs.   (The **cats sleep**.)

    (3) Compound subjects joined by *and* take a plural verb.
       (The **cat** and the **dog are** sleeping.)

    (4) When compound subjects are joined by *or* or *nor*, the verb agrees with the subject nearer the verb.
       (The **cats** or the **dog is** sleeping. The **dog** or the **cats are** sleeping.)

When the subject follows the verb, find the subject. Then, make sure that the verb agrees with it.
    ([Is, Are] the cats sleeping? The cats [is, are] sleeping? The **cats are** sleeping. **Are** the **cats** sleeping?)

When a sentence has a verb phrase, the first helping verb in the phrase agrees with the subject.
    (The **cats are** sleeping.)

The number of a subject is not changed by a phrase following the subject.
    (The **cats** in the kitchen **are** sleeping.)

The following indefinite pronouns are singular: *anybody, anyone, each, either, everybody, everyone, nobody, neither, no one, one, somebody,* and *someone*.
    (**Each** of the cats **is** sleeping.)

The following indefinite pronouns are plural: *both, few, many,* and *several*.
    (**Several** of the cats **are** sleeping.)

The number of the indefinite pronouns *all, any, most, none,* and *some* is determined by the number of the object in the prepositional phrase following the subject. If the pronoun refers to a singular object, the pronoun is singular. If the pronoun refers to a plural object, the pronoun is plural.
    (**Most** of the **cats are** sleeping. **Most** of their **food is** gone.)

SUMMARY OF USES OF THE COMMA

Use commas to separate items in a series.

    (1) If all items in a series are joined by *and* or *or,* do not use commas to separate them.

    (2) Independent clauses in a series are usually separated by semicolons. Short independent clauses, however, may be separated by commas.

Use commas to separate two or more adjectives preceding a noun.

Use commas before *and, but, or, nor, for, so,* and *yet* when they join independent clauses.

Use commas to set off nonessential clauses and nonessential participial phrases.

Use commas after certain introductory elements.

    (1) Use a comma after words such as *well, yes, no,* and *why* when they begin a sentence.

    (2) Use a comma after an introductory participle or participial phrase.

    (3) Use a comma after a series of introductory prepositional phrases.

    (4) Use a comma after an introductory adverb clause.

Use commas to set off sentence interrupters.

    (1) Appositives and appositive phrases are usually set off by commas.

    (2) Words used in direct address are set off by commas.

    (3) Parenthetical expressions are set off by commas.

Use commas in certain conventional situations.

    (1) Use a comma to separate items in dates and addresses.

    (2) Use a comma after the salutation of a friendly letter and after the closing of any letter.

    (3) Use a comma after a name followed by an abbreviation such as *Jr., Sr.,* and *M.D.*

Do not use unnecessary commas.

Chapter 1: The Parts of a Sentence, pp. 1–6

Sentences and Sentence Fragments, pp. 1–2

Exercise A
1. When will the next train leave?
2. The class planted ten new trees.
3. Look at those stars!
4. What a wonderful play that was!
5. Has my letter arrived yet?

Exercise B
6. F
7. F
8. S
9. S
10. F

Exercise C
Answers will vary. Sample responses are provided.
11. Lucinda sent an e-mail to her cousin.
12. After the car has been washed, we will go for a ride.
13. Carlos threw a long touchdown pass.
14. J.R.R. Tolkien was a terrific writer!
15. What was the final score?

The Subject, pp. 3–4

Exercise A
1. Throughout the solar system are <u>nine planets</u>.
2. Just before sunrise and just after sunset, <u>planets</u> are visible.
3. With a telescope, <u>you</u> can see Saturn's rings.
4. <u>Pictures of the Martian landscape</u> may amaze you.
5. <u>Two satellites</u> orbit the planet Mars.

Exercise B
6. <u>Many colorful balloons</u> floated above the dance floor.
7. When are <u>the Connors</u> moving to Arizona?
8. <u>Dust</u> covered the furniture in the old house.
9. Above the sofa in the den hangs <u>a painting of a country landscape</u>.
10. Did <u>you</u> speak to Evan about our plans for tonight?

Exercise C
11. <u>Noel</u> and <u>Kendall</u> are starring in the play.
12. <u>Sweaters</u> or <u>jackets</u> are on sale this week.
13. Are <u>maps</u>, <u>dictionaries</u>, and <u>encyclopedias</u> in the reference section?
14. Under the rug were <u>dust</u> and <u>dirt</u>.
15. During the open house, <u>parents</u> and <u>relatives</u> viewed the students' work.

The Predicate, pp. 5–6

Exercise A
1. The crunchy cereal <u>suddenly popped</u>!
2. Each piece of cereal <u>contained starch</u>.
3. <u>Inside the starch were</u> air pockets.
4. <u>In the milk</u>, the starch <u>became wet</u>.
5. The air pockets <u>then exploded with a pop</u>.

Exercise B
6. Katie <u>reads books about science fiction and adventure</u>.
7. Michelle <u>has never been a judge for the art contest</u>.
8. <u>Before the soccer game</u>, the players <u>stretched</u>.
9. <u>Through the dense forest bends</u> a narrow, rippling brook.
10. <u>Were</u> the children <u>laughing at the silly cartoon</u>?

Exercise C
11. We <u>enjoyed</u> our family vacation and <u>will remember</u> it fondly.
12. My older brother Carlos <u>surfed</u> the big waves or <u>read</u> a book.

13. I <u>fished</u> a few times but <u>caught</u> nothing.
14. In the evenings, we <u>took</u> walks, <u>told</u> stories, or <u>sang</u> songs.
15. <u>Will</u> your family <u>go</u> to the beach this summer or <u>hike</u> in the mountains?

Chapter 2: Parts of Speech Overview: Noun, Pronoun, Adjective, pp. 7–16

The Noun, pp. 7–8

EXERCISE A

1. Will Hobbs has written many great books for young readers.
2. What excitement the children in the stories experience!
3. In *Ghost Canoe*, Nathan MacAllister investigates a shipwreck.
4. Nathan and his mother live with the Makah Indians near the Pacific Ocean.
5. After a ship crashes on the rocks near the shore, strange events occur.
6. Who is the wild, hairy man that is hiding in the caves?
7. Captain Bim, a neighbor, buries treasures during the night.
8. A skeleton in an old canoe is discovered in a strange place: high in a tree.
9. Nathan and Lighthouse George search for clues to these mysteries.
10. Nathan shows great bravery and self-reliance during his adventure.

EXERCISE B

11. Gloria and Christina Santos had first planned the trip to the mall.
12. At the last minute, Christina couldn't go.
13. Gloria called Marcus, who lives nearby on Shepherd Lane.
14. Mrs. Byrd took both friends to the mall.
15. First, Gloria wanted to look at sneakers at Foot Market.
16. Next, she and Marcus browsed through the books, maps, and magazines at Skyline Bookstore.
17. Gloria found a fantastic book on the solar system.
18. Later, the two teenagers met Mrs. Byrd at the food court.
19. The book gave the girl self-confidence for her speech on the planets the next week.
20. The book was definitely cited in her report for Ms. Saunders.

Personal, Reflexive, and Intensive Pronouns, pp. 9–10

EXERCISE A

1. Chapbooks got their name from the chapmen who sold them.
2. Have you heard of chapmen?
3. They traveled around and sold chapbooks.
4. People bought inexpensive chapbooks for their own entertainment.
5. A chapbook was small; its pages measured approximately five inches by four inches.
6. A person could read about his or her favorite hero in a chapbook.
7. Ms. Williams told us about the jokes, rhymes, and stories in chapbooks.
8. The students said, "We will make our own chapbooks."
9. All students will collect their stories in a chapbook.
10. Lucinda and I asked to put pictures in our chapbooks.

EXERCISE B

11. REF
12. INT
13. INT
14. REF
15. REF
16. INT
17. REF
18. INT
19. REF
20. REF

Developmental Language Skills Answer Key

Demonstrative and Relative Pronouns, pp. 11–12

Exercise A
1. That
2. This
3. that
4. these
5. Those
6. These
7. that
8. This
9. These
10. those

Exercise B
11. REL
12. DEM
13. REL
14. REL
15. DEM
16. REL
17. DEM
18. REL
19. DEM
20. DEM

Indefinite and Interrogative Pronouns, pp. 13–14

Exercise A
1. Everybody
2. Several
3. each
4. Somebody
5. Few
6. All
7. None
8. some
9. None
10. Each

Exercise B
11. INTER
12. IND
13. INTER
14. IND
15. INTER
16. IND
17. IND
18. IND
19. INTER
20. IND

The Adjective, pp. 15–16

Exercise A
1. <u>Many</u> people have a cat or a dog as a pet.
2. Cody, however, has a <u>white</u> rabbit as a pet.
3. The <u>small</u> rabbit lives in a <u>large</u> pen in the bedroom.
4. A <u>tiny</u> doghouse serves as a <u>cozy</u> burrow for the rabbit.
5. Cody gives Thumper <u>clean</u> water <u>every</u> day.
6. Thumper eats <u>fresh</u> vegetables and <u>special</u> food for rabbits.
7. On <u>quiet</u> afternoons, Cody lets Thumper out of the pen.
8. Cody likes to pet the <u>silky</u>, <u>soft</u> fur that Thumper has.
9. During the <u>short</u> playtimes, Cody keeps Thumper away from <u>dangerous</u> places.
10. Thumper seems to enjoy the <u>extra</u> attention.

Exercise B
11. An <u>empty</u> cabin sat in a <u>small</u> meadow.
12. Nearby, the <u>rapid</u> river rushed between <u>muddy</u> banks.
13. The hikers, <u>hungry</u> and <u>weary</u>, stopped in the meadow.
14. They looked at the <u>ancient</u> bridge and <u>deep</u> water.
15. They wondered how they had gotten to the <u>remote</u>, <u>lonely</u> place.
16. The <u>correct</u> path through the woods wasn't <u>clear</u>.
17. <u>One</u> hiker, <u>smart</u> and <u>practical</u>, built a <u>warm</u> fire.
18. The <u>other</u> person unfolded a <u>large</u> map of the area.
19. One of them pulled a <u>small</u> compass and <u>extra</u> food from a backpack.
20. They ate food and drank <u>fresh</u> water, and they plotted a <u>clear</u> course home.

Exercise C

[21] As Juanita dribbled the basketball, her <u>new</u> sneakers squeaked. [22] She pretended to step <u>one</u> way, then changed directions at the <u>last</u> second. [23] An <u>unlucky</u> opponent tried to stop Juanita, but could not. [24] Juanita shot the ball and made an <u>easy</u> basket. [25] The <u>smooth</u> ball barely touched the net as it flew through the air.

Chapter 3: Parts of Speech Overview, pp. 17–26

The Verb, pp. 17–18

Exercise A
1. walked
2. were
3. looked
4. stood
5. was
6. belonged
7. put
8. brings
9. is
10. give

Exercise B
11. What information could Toby find about Nebraska?
12. He had been studying an atlas.
13. Do you know the history of Nebraska's name?
14. The Oto Indians had named one of the rivers *Nebrathka*.
15. Today, this river is known as the Platte River.
16. We have taken the name for Nebraska from *Nebrathka*.
17. Toby was finding other facts.
18. For instance, Buffalo Bill had made his home in Nebraska.
19. A large mammoth fossil had been found in the southwestern area of the state.
20. Arbor Day was begun by a Nebraskan, Julius Sterling Morton.

Action Verbs and Linking Verbs, pp. 19–20

Exercise A
1. Thorns grow on the stem of a rose.
2. Did the newspaper staff meet their deadline?
3. We named our new puppy Peanuts.
4. The flowers are blooming now.
5. Did you volunteer at the food bank?
6. The history students have not presented their reports yet.
7. On winter evenings, the farmer feeds hay to his cows.
8. Ms. Kaufmann's secretary has a message for her.
9. We have formed a plan for the autumn carnival.
10. On the bus, we usually talk about friends and activities.

Exercise B
11. Lee will be Aunt Juanita's assistant this summer.
12. Aunt Juanita is a landscape architect.
13. Photographs of her designs are special features in many landscaping magazines.
14. Her business has become a great success.
15. She was extremely busy last year.
16. Her designs look unique.
17. Has anyone ever been unhappy with her work?
18. Her backyard is a work of art.
19. Does the flowing water sound peaceful to you?
20. The flowers and herbs smell wonderful.

The Adverb, pp. 21–22

Exercise A
1. recently
2. carefully
3. very
4. often
5. quite
6. Sometimes

7. there
8. really
9. probably
10. already

EXERCISE B
11. My family seldom travels out of state.
12. Did all the balloons float away?
13. The gymnast can easily perform his routines.
14. Richard was slowly pronouncing the words in German.
15. My brother is rarely sick.
16. Will your sister attend college soon?
17. He has memorized nearly all his lines for the school play.
18. I hardly recognized my cousin at the family reunion.
19. That movie was really funny!
20. We had not read *The View from Saturday*.

The Preposition, pp. 23–24
EXERCISE A
1. by
2. beside
3. on
4. inside
5. into, on
6. After, on
7. on
8. Behind
9. against
10. for

EXERCISE B
11. Aside from
12. underneath
13. out of
14. in place of
15. next to
16. due to
17. next to
18. throughout
19. In addition to
20. with

The Conjunction and the Interjection, pp. 25–26
EXERCISE A
1. and
2. yet
3. and
4. so
5. nor

EXERCISE B
6. Not only . . . but also
7. Either . . . or
8. Both . . . and
9. whether . . . or
10. Neither . . . nor

EXERCISE C
11. Hurray
12. oh
13. Aw
14. Whew
15. Goodness

Chapter 4: The Phrase and the Clause, pp. 27–42

The Prepositional Phrase, pp. 27–28

EXERCISE A
1. P
2. P
3. NP
4. P
5. NP
6. P
7. P
8. NP
9. P
10. P

EXERCISE B
11. Its trunk leans <u>toward one side or the other</u>.
12. This tree is usually found <u>near sandy beaches</u>.
13. <u>In addition to green palm leaves</u>, the tree produces coconuts.
14. Have you ever bought a whole coconut <u>from a store or market</u>?
15. <u>Inside the husk and shell</u> is the nut itself.
16. The nut resembles a white ball <u>with a hollow center</u>.
17. <u>Within the center</u>, the nut holds coconut milk.
18. Some people use the milk <u>in special recipes</u>.
19. Others drain the milk <u>into the sink</u> and then eat the nut.
20. I enjoy fresh, sweet coconut <u>as a snack</u>.

The Adjective Phrase, pp. 29–30

EXERCISE A
1. The food <u>from the vendor</u> was delicious.
2. We entered the tent <u>with the big top</u>.
3. Are some <u>of the front seats</u> still available?
4. The trapeze artists <u>near the ladder</u> are extremely talented!
5. Watch the man <u>on the unicycle</u>.
6. A group <u>of teenage performers</u> entered the center ring.
7. Is the one <u>in the black outfit</u> their team captain?
8. A large crowd <u>of people</u> were watching a juggler.
9. The hall <u>of mirrors</u> looks fun.
10. Try the game <u>with the silver rings</u>.

EXERCISE B
11. The name <u>of the main character</u> is Puck.
12. The story recounts Puck's trip <u>to another part</u> <u>of the universe</u>.
13. When she leaves school, the adventures <u>of Puck</u> truly begin.
14. Puck's parents are studying life <u>on another planet</u>.
15. Her best friend <u>on the ship</u> is Hush, an alien.
16. Together, they must solve the theft <u>of a valuable piece</u> <u>of art</u>.
17. Some police <u>on the ship</u> are working undercover.
18. Don't a number <u>of alien ghosts</u> haunt the ship?
19. Puck is the hero <u>of this memorable story</u>.
20. She displays the wisdom <u>of a much older person</u>.

The Adverb Phrase, pp. 31–32
Exercise A
1. The fans clapped <u>with enthusiasm</u>.
2. Cedric dropped a penny <u>into the fountain</u>.
3. This box is full <u>of old clothes</u>.
4. <u>After the concert</u> we ate frozen yogurt.
5. Wow! Jack caught the fly ball <u>with one hand</u>.
6. Decorate the bulletin board <u>with paper snowflakes</u>.
7. Nina was early <u>for her dentist appointment</u>.
8. High <u>in the mountains</u> is a beautiful waterfall.
9. Had everyone arrived <u>before Keith</u>?
10. <u>Around my ears</u> buzzed a hungry mosquito.

Exercise B
11. <u>During the summer</u> the heat grew fierce.
12. Then, Carlos told us <u>about the new ice rink</u>.
13. Has the ice rink opened <u>to the public</u>?
14. <u>During the afternoon</u> we went <u>to the ice rink</u>.
15. Rent your ice skates <u>at the front desk</u>.
16. <u>As a child</u>, I had skated <u>on ice</u> a few times.
17. <u>At the rink</u> we enjoyed ourselves <u>on the ice</u>.
18. My brother Raul has always been good <u>at skating</u>.
19. Did you bring gloves <u>with you</u> <u>to the rink</u>?
20. Follow me <u>across the ice</u>.

The Clause, pp. 33–34
Exercise A
1. IND
2. Not
3. Not
4. IND
5. Not
6. IND
7. IND
8. Not
9. Not
10. IND

Exercise B
11. SUB
12. SUB
13. IND
14. SUB
15. IND

The Adjective Clause, pp. 35–36
Exercise A
1. The last entertainer <u>that performed</u> was named Suzi.
2. Look up the word in the dictionary, <u>which is on the desk</u>.
3. Jim quickly wrote out the math problems <u>that the teacher had assigned</u>.
4. Have you learned some skills <u>that help you on tests</u>?
5. Is Marian one of the students <u>whose grades have improved</u>?
6. The students <u>who sit in the front row</u> will be team captains.
7. Let's listen to Rosa, <u>who composed a piece of music for the concert</u>.
8. You might be interested in an idea <u>that Antonio had</u>.
9. The girl <u>whose essay won the contest</u> was happy.
10. David crossed out each choice <u>that was incorrect</u>.

Exercise B
11. Katrina, <u>whom I met at band camp</u>, is marching in the parade.
12. Have you seen the baseball player <u>whose cap is on backward</u>?

13. The quizzes, <u>which Ms. Wood will grade this afternoon</u>, will be returned tomorrow.
14. The students will send a valentine to everyone <u>that is in their class</u>.
15. Sign up anyone <u>who has a student identification card</u>.
16. Was the player <u>who hit the home run</u> Shannon?
17. The hose <u>that connected the radiator</u> had come loose.
18. Give a program to everyone <u>who comes in this door</u>.
19. My parents had offered me good advice, <u>which I followed</u>.
20. The winner of this game is the one <u>who gets the fewest points</u>.

The Adverb Clause, pp. 37–38
Exercise A
1. I wasn't hungry at lunch (because) I had eaten a late breakfast.
2. (Unless) Tina knows the answer, her team will not win.
3. (Before) I drank the water, I squeezed a lemon into it.
4. Don't call Chen (until) you get home.
5. Alex closed his eyes (while) he thought about a topic for his paper.
6. Willis will take lessons (until) he joins a tennis league.
7. (If) you run in the relay race, will you be the first runner on your team?
8. The second loaf of bread cooked faster (than) the first loaf did.
9. (When) the light rain started, several frogs began jumping near the grassy area.
10. Candles have been providing light to the room (since) the power went out.

Exercise B
11. <u>While I'm visiting my cousins</u>, we will go to a tennis tournament.
12. My room will be completely clean <u>if I spend only one hour cleaning it</u>.
13. <u>After Lucinda studied</u>, she took her dog Lester for a walk.
14. Please tell me about the party <u>before you leave</u>.
15. <u>Unless we go to the post office now</u>, the package will be late.
16. <u>As long as you are going to the store</u>, will you buy some milk?
17. We brought a sack lunch to eat <u>while we are on the field trip</u>.
18. Help me lift this chair <u>so that we can move it over there</u>.
19. Doesn't Steve write poetry <u>when he has some spare time</u>?
20. <u>Before you turn in your assignment</u>, make sure you have written your name on it.

Simple Sentences and Compound Sentences, pp. 39–40
Exercise A
1. <u>Aunt Leona</u> <u>has worked</u> as a pilot for fifteen years.
2. As a teenager, <u>she</u> <u>dreamed</u> of a future in the sky.
3. With her goals in mind, <u>she</u> <u>saved</u> money.
4. Later, <u>Aunt Leona</u> <u>paid</u> for her own flying lessons.
5. <u>Have</u> <u>you</u> ever <u>traveled</u> in a plane or jet?

EXERCISE B

6. The <u>librarian</u> and the <u>teacher</u> <u>are showing</u> a video in the library.
7. In the evening, <u>Cedric</u> <u>reads</u> a book or <u>writes</u> in his journal.
8. Please <u>call</u> Samantha and <u>ask</u> her to join our team. *(you)*
9. <u>Alfredo</u> and his <u>brother</u> <u>stood</u> in front of the building.
10. <u>Did</u> <u>you</u> <u>walk</u> the dog and <u>give</u> him a bath?

EXERCISE C

<u>CD</u> 11. Carlos volunteers at the library, and he goes there once a week.
<u>S</u> 12. Does he help out with Story Hour each Saturday afternoon?
<u>CD</u> 13. Many young children attend, for they enjoy a good tale.
<u>CD</u> 14. Watch the children's faces; they are very funny.
<u>S</u> 15. They laugh and scream with delight at the stories.

Complex Sentences and Compound-Complex Sentences, pp. 41–42

EXERCISE A

1. <u>Spiffy,</u> <u>who is a golden retriever,</u> <u>is</u> always <u>cheerful.</u>
2. <u>He greets me joyfully at the door</u> <u>as soon as I get home.</u>
3. <u>I usually play with him in the yard</u> <u>after I put my backpack in my room.</u>
4. <u>Before he will catch the ball,</u> <u>Spiffy likes to run around the yard a few times.</u>
5. <u>Spiffy always jumps high</u> <u>whenever I throw the ball.</u>

EXERCISE B

6. CD-CX
7. CD-CX
8. CX
9. CX
10. CD-CX

Chapter 5: Complements, pp. 43–46

Direct Objects and Indirect Objects, pp. 43–44

Exercise A

1. The <u>hammer</u> <u>drove</u> the (nail) into the plywood.
2. My <u>uncle</u> <u>visited</u> (Miami) last year.
3. The <u>youth group</u> <u>cleaned</u> the (shed) for Mrs. Nelson.
4. <u>May</u> <u>I</u> <u>pay</u> the (bill) with a check?
5. In her younger days, my <u>grandmother</u> <u>won</u> many swimming (contests).

Exercise B

6. The sixth-graders were making <u>posters</u>.
7. Lupita was using special <u>tape</u>.
8. First, she stuck the <u>tape</u> onto her poster.
9. Next, she pulled the <u>backing</u> from the other side of the tape.
10. Finally, she sprinkled <u>beads</u> and <u>glitter</u> onto the sticky surface.

Exercise C

11. Please show (me) your new <u>outfit</u>.
12. The counselor told the (campers) some important <u>advice</u>.
13. Kris has given the (bookshelf) a new <u>coat</u> of paint.
14. After the game, the team promised (itself) and its (fans) a victory <u>party</u>.
15. Did the waiter bring (you) that <u>menu</u>?

Predicate Nominatives and Predicate Adjectives, pp. 45–46

Exercise A

1. The leader of the food drive <u>is</u> (Amanda).
2. <u>Was</u> the dog in that commercial a (collie)?
3. My favorite color <u>is</u> (green).
4. Last <u>year</u>, the organizer of the book fair <u>was</u> (Leena Benson).
5. That tall building <u>is the</u> (Empire State Building).

Exercise B

6. These roses <u>smell</u> (sweet).
7. My sister <u>stays</u> (calm) in a crisis.
8. <u>Are</u> the floors (wet) from the detergent?
9. One actor <u>looked</u> (nervous).
10. The soup at the restaurant <u>was too</u> (hot).

Exercise C

_PN_ 11. Was the winner of the prize your <u>aunt</u> or your <u>uncle</u>?

_PA_ 12. The fairgrounds were <u>bright</u> and <u>attractive</u>.

_PN_ 13. Our snack was <u>peanuts</u> and <u>juice</u>.

_PA_ 14. The line for the bumper cars was <u>long</u> and <u>slow</u>.

_PN_ 15. Are the three people in the background <u>Tim Vinson</u>, <u>Ed Garcia</u>, and <u>Cindy Spencer</u>?

Chapter 6: Agreement, pp. 47–56

Subject-Verb Agreement, pp. 47–48

EXERCISE A
1. stops
2. make
3. sleeps
4. bring
5. hangs

EXERCISE B
6. come
7. give
8. use
9. reflect
10. become

EXERCISE C
11. are
12. Does
13. Have
14. Is
15. have

Subject-Verb Agreement: Indefinite Pronouns, pp. 49–50

EXERCISE A
1. is
2. contains
3. has
4. helps
5. wakes

EXERCISE B
6. have
7. lock
8. hang
9. have
10. are

EXERCISE C
11. Some of the carrots (is, *are*) already sliced.
12. None of the test (*seems*, seem) difficult.
13. All of the apples (tastes, *taste*) delicious.
14. More of the wheat (are, *is*) stored in the grain bin.
15. Any of these books (*interest*, interests) me.

Subject-Verb Agreement: Compound Subjects, pp. 51–52

EXERCISE A
1. get
2. remind
3. are
4. Do
5. wake

EXERCISE B
6. drives
7. stay
8. Have
9. belongs
10. Does

EXERCISE C
11. come
12. was
13. is
14. clear
15. were

Pronoun-Antecedent Agreement A, pp. 53–54

EXERCISE A
1. her
2. his
3. he
4. it
5. her

EXERCISE B
6. its
7. them
8. them
9. their
10. them

EXERCISE C
11. their
12. their
13. her
14. their
15. its

Pronoun-Antecedent Agreement B, pp. 55–56

EXERCISE A
1. its
2. his or her
3. its
4. his or her
5. his

EXERCISE B
6. their
7. their
8. their
9. their
10. their

EXERCISE C
11. Most of my baseball cards have kept (its, **their**) value.
12. Most of this metal box has rust on (**it**, them).
13. Have some of your old coins lost (its, **their**) shine?
14. Any of these nickels will shine if you polish (it, **them**).
15. Does any of the bread have oats in (**it**, them)?

Developmental Language Skills Answer Key

Chapter 7: Using Verbs Correctly, pp. 57–72

Principal Parts of Verbs, pp. 57–58

EXERCISE A
1. past
2. past participle
3. past
4. present participle
5. past participle
6. base form
7. past participle
8. present participle
9. past
10. base form

EXERCISE B
11. won
12. measured
13. colored
14. known
15. planning
16. studied
17. helped
18. adding
19. building
20. used

Regular Verbs, pp. 59–60

EXERCISE A
1. placed
2. bothering
3. supposed
4. liked
5. researched
6. dreamed
7. remained
8. used
9. decided
10. watching

EXERCISE B
11. skipped
12. tried
13. hoping
14. supposed
15. occurred
16. stunned
17. recycling
18. mapped
19. providing
20. trotted

Irregular Verbs A, pp. 61–62

EXERCISE A
1. lent
2. had
3. made
4. spent
5. lost
6. heard
7. lent
8. lost
9. made
10. had

EXERCISE B
11. lost
12. made
13. sent
14. had
15. lent
16. heard
17. spent
18. made
19. lost
20. had

Irregular Verbs B, pp. 63–64

EXERCISE A
1. swam
2. come
3. rang
4. ran
5. led
6. sank
7. shrunk

8. held
9. drank
10. began

EXERCISE B
11. swum
12. led
13. sung
14. came
15. began
16. held
17. became
18. shrunk
19. sunk
20. run

Irregular Verbs C, pp. 65–66
EXERCISE A
1. ridden
2. left
3. said
4. drawn
5. gone
6. froze
7. stood
8. taken
9. eaten
10. written

EXERCISE B
11. cut
12. sung
13. read
14. put
15. cut
16. burst
17. held
18. hit
19. ran
20. drank

Verb Tense, pp. 67–68
EXERCISE A
1. past
2. present
3. present perfect
4. present
5. past

EXERCISE B
6. future
7. past perfect
8. future
9. future perfect
10. past perfect

EXERCISE C
11. will feature
12. are collecting
13. drives
14. bumped
15. had visited

Sit and *Set*; *Rise* and *Raise*; *Lie* and *Lay* A, pp. 69–70
EXERCISE A
1. sat
2. setting
3. sit
4. set
5. set

EXERCISE B
6. rising
7. rose
8. raise
9. rose
10. raised

EXERCISE C
11. lay
12. lay
13. lain
14. laid
15. lies

Developmental Language Skills Answer Key

Sit and Set; Rise and Raise; Lie and Lay B, pp. 71–72

EXERCISE A
1. Sit
2. set
3. set
4. sitting
5. sit

EXERCISE B
6. raised
7. raise
8. rises
9. raise
10. rose

EXERCISE C
11. lying
12. lie
13. lay
14. laid
15. lay

Chapter 8: Using Pronouns Correctly, pp. 73–80

The Forms of Personal Pronouns, pp. 73–74

EXERCISE A
1. We started a new project today.
2. Do you have any pets?
3. The pitcher during the second inning was she.
4. Once I saw a bald eagle.
5. Are they coming to see the school play?

EXERCISE B
6. Jonathan gave me a calendar.
7. Mario told her about the trip to Florida.
8. The Smiths always take the dog with them on vacation.
9. Was the delivery for us?
10. Claudia drew a picture of him.

EXERCISE C
Answers will vary. Sample responses are provided.
11. I often misplace ___my___ house key.
12. Is this blue sweater ___his___?
13. Our dog Buck searched all over the house for ___its___ favorite toy.
14. Sarah keeps ___her___ sketches in a large folder.
15. The cast members looked wonderful in ___their___ costumes.

The Subject Form, pp. 75–76

EXERCISE A
1. he
2. she
3. I
4. they
5. he

EXERCISE B
6. they
7. she
8. he
9. I
10. he
11. we
12. she
13. he
14. he
15. they

The Object Form, pp. 77–78

EXERCISE A
1. us
2. me
3. her
4. him
5. them

EXERCISE B
6. me
7. her
8. us
9. him
10. us

EXERCISE C
11. her
12. us
13. him
14. him
15. whom

Special Pronoun Problems, pp. 79–80

EXERCISE A
1. We
2. us
3. us
4. we
5. We

EXERCISE B
6. Whom
7. Who
8. whom
9. who
10. whom

Developmental Language Skills Answer Key

EXERCISE C
11. Whom
12. We
13. us
14. Who
15. whom
16. we
17. Who
18. us
19. we
20. whom

Chapter 9: Using Modifiers Correctly, pp. 81–90

Forms of Modifiers, pp. 81–82

Exercise A

1. ADJ
2. ADV
3. ADJ
4. ADV
5. ADV

Exercise B

6. ADV
7. ADJ
8. ADV
9. ADJ
10. ADJ
11. ADJ
12. ADV
13. ADJ
14. ADV
15. ADV

Degrees of Comparison, pp. 83–84

Exercise A

1. superlative
2. positive
3. comparative
4. comparative
5. superlative

Exercise B

POSITIVE	COMPARATIVE	SUPERLATIVE
6. colorful	more colorful	most colorful
7. sensitive	more sensitive	most sensitive
8. gently	more gently	most gently
9. brave	braver	bravest
10. often	more often	most often
11. weak	weaker	weakest
12. thoughtful	more thoughtful	most thoughtful
13. creatively	more creatively	most creatively
14. witty	wittier	wittiest
15. awkwardly	more awkwardly	most awkwardly

Regular and Irregular Comparison, pp. 85–86

Exercise A

1. more loudly
2. livelier [*or* more lively]
3. most capably
4. least sturdy
5. more rapidly

Exercise B

6. worse
7. More
8. better
9. better
10. more
11. worst
12. most
13. more
14. best
15. best

Special Problems in Using Modifiers, pp. 87–88

Exercise A

1. My headache feels (worser) this afternoon than this morning. ___worse___
2. Which trees in the park are the (most tallest)? ___tallest___
3. The movie ended (more sooner) than I expected. ___sooner___
4. Venus is the (most brightest) planet in the nighttime sky. ___brightest___
5. Who gave Mrs. Wilkins her (most favoritest) book? ___most favorite___
6. The ostrich can grow (more larger) than the emu. ___larger___
7. I like spinach (more better) than I like broccoli. ___better___
8. The damage to the car is (worser) than I thought. ___worse___

Developmental Language Skills Answer Key

9. Did Melissa write the (bestest) essay on trees?
   _____best_____

10. Our lawn is (more greener) than our neighbor's lawn. _____greener_____

EXERCISE B

Some answers may vary.

11. Don't leave any wet clothes on the floor.
12. Hardly anybody showed up for the rally.
13. We will never forget Mr. Major's kindness.
14. The Sanchezes had scarcely finished dinner when the doorbell rang.
15. Even though the show was over, no one went anywhere.

Placement of Modifiers, pp. 89–90

EXERCISE A

1. Leonardo da Vinci <u>nearly</u> painted the *Mona Lisa* five hundred years ago.
2. We watched a film that was directed by Ron Howard <u>today</u>.
3. Some sunflowers <u>almost</u> grow up to fifteen feet high.
4. Josh and I visited some ruins left by ancient American Indians <u>last week</u>.
5. <u>Overhead</u>, we watched as the balloon sailed into the sky.

EXERCISE B

6. Mrs. Palmer lives down the street <u>who drives a convertible</u>.
7. Leslie said <u>during lunch</u> she would try out for the school play. *or* <u>during lunch</u> . . . the school play.
8. Some pennies were made during World War II <u>of steel</u>.
9. The fish is swimming in the bowl <u>with a gold tail</u>.
10. Delores sends greeting cards to her friends <u>that she makes herself</u>.

Chapter 10: A Glossary of Usage, pp. 91–94

Glossary of Usage A, pp. 91–92

Exercise A

1. excepted
2. somewhere
3. accept
4. Isn't
5. excepted
6. aren't
7. except
8. everywhere
9. accept
10. except

Exercise B

11. bad
12. between
13. badly
14. among
15. bad
16. among
17. badly
18. between
19. bad
20. among

Glossary of Usage B, pp. 93–94

Exercise A

1. fewer
2. could have
3. less
4. should have
5. fewer
6. less
7. might have
8. less
9. ought to have
10. fewer

Exercise B

11. than
12. teach
13. then
14. supposed to
15. taught
16. then
17. supposed to
18. learning
19. than
20. than

Chapter 11: Capital Letters, pp. 95–104

First Words; Letter Salutations and Closings; The Pronoun *I*, pp. 95–96

EXERCISE A

1. **H**ave you ever seen a mummy?
2. **T**he mummies in this museum are from Egypt.
3. **S**ome mummies have been found in Peru.
4. **M**any objects were buried with the mummies.
5. **S**ometimes robbers broke into the burial places.

EXERCISE B

6. "**C**an your father give us a ride?" asked Sam.
7. Susanna said, "**Y**es, I think he can."
8. "**M**y brother can pick us up after the movie," said Sam.
9. "**D**oes he have his own car?" asked Susanna.
10. Sam said, "**N**o, he drives my parents' car."

EXERCISE C

11. **M**y dear Aunt Mary,
12. **Y**ours truly,
13. **D**ear Mom and Dad,
14. **S**incerely,
15. **D**ear Mr. Jacobs:

EXERCISE D

16. Let's see if **I**'ve got two dollars.
17. Do you think **I** can ride with you?
18. What time do **I** have to be home?
19. He forgot that **I**'d already walked the dog.
20. May **I** sit here, please?

Proper Nouns A, pp. 97–98

EXERCISE A

1. West Virginia
2. California
3. his dog Pooch
4. Anita Simpson
5. in August

EXERCISE B

6. My father's name is **L**awrence **B**. **J**ohnson.
7. Are **R**ita and **A**nna at school today?
8. Here is a biography of **F**lorence **N**ightingale.
9. I think you will enjoy **E**. **L**. **K**onigsburg's books.
10. The name of our new puppy is **G**oldie.

EXERCISE C

11. He is a well-known ~~P~~rofessor.
12. Our guest speaker today is **M**ajor Katherine Gibbs.
13. Have you met **M**r. and **M**rs. Gonzales?
14. I have an appointment with the ~~D~~octor this afternoon.
15. Her report is about **P**resident Carter.

EXERCISE D

16. You should send your ~~A~~unt Emily a birthday card.
17. I am helping **D**ad paint the fence.
18. My ~~C~~ousins Joe and Kevin have new bicycles.
19. Your father and **G**randpa Jefferson are in the backyard.
20. Did **U**ncle Raymond call this afternoon?

Proper Nouns B, pp. 99–100

EXERCISE A

1. Frank has lived in **B**razil and **C**osta **R**ica.
2. Does the **M**ississippi **R**iver flow through **M**issouri?
3. The river empties into the **G**ulf of **M**exico near **N**ew **O**rleans.

4. Many people have climbed mount everest.
5. My family saw the bats at carlsbad caverns national park.
6. The ancient city of athens is still the capital of greece.
7. In 1927, Charles Lindbergh made the first solo flight across the atlantic ocean.
8. When you come to the first stoplight, turn west onto broad street.
9. The world's largest desert is on the continent of africa.
10. The capital city of california is sacramento.

Exercise B

11. This publication is from the american heart association.
12. The bears and the hornets are playing at the stadium today.
13. My sister has applied to georgetown university.
14. We went on a field trip to the los angeles county museum of art.
15. The river city high school rockets are in the playoffs this year.

Exercise C

16. Each state elects two members of the u.s. senate.
17. She works for the fbi in Washington, D.C.
18. The madison city council will meet tomorrow afternoon.
19. This bank is insured by the fdic (federal deposit insurance corporation).
20. We will visit the headquarters of the united nations in New York.

Proper Nouns C, pp. 101–102

Exercise A

1. Let's volunteer to help with the special olympics.
2. On presidents' day we honor the birthdays of George Washington and Abraham Lincoln.
3. Joe has practice after school on wednesday.
4. My family always goes to the beach in july.
5. The dark ages followed the collapse of the Roman Empire.

Exercise B

6. A major religion in India is hinduism.
7. Does your family celebrate christmas?
8. Her great-grandparents are italian.
9. The maya built an amazing civilization in southern Mexico and Central America.
10. The jewish celebration of passover takes place in March or April each year.

Exercise C

11. The white house is at 1600 Pennsylvania Avenue.
12. Shuttle flights were stopped for several years after the explosion of the challenger in 1986.
13. Everyone has heard about the sinking of the titanic.
14. Abraham Lincoln was shot while he was watching a performance at ford's theatre.
15. The statue of liberty was a gift to the United States from France.

Exercise D

16. The smallest planet is mercury.
17. The bright stars pollux and castor are in the constellation gemini.

18. The nearest spiral galaxy to our own is andromeda.
19. The first recorded sightings of halley's comet were made about 240 B.C.
20. Can you find the group of stars called the big dipper?

Titles of Creative Works, pp. 103–104

EXERCISE A

1. Last weekend we watched the movie *north by northwest*.
2. The orchestra played *tales from the vienna woods*, by Johann Strauss.
3. This is a photograph of *bronco buster*, a sculpture by Frederic Remington.
4. I found an article about bicycles in *outdoor life*.
5. Reporters from the *arkansas democrat-gazette* covered the story.
6. Arthur Miller's play *death of a salesman* won a Pulitzer.
7. The class has been reading Hemingway's *the old man and the sea*.
8. This painting is called *early sunday morning*.
9. My sister found the recipe in an old issue of *good housekeeping*.
10. Charles Dickens' book *a christmas carol* has been made into a movie many times.

EXERCISE B

11. Almost everyone has finished reading O. Henry's story "the gift of the magi."
12. "stopping by woods on a snowy evening" is a well-known poem by Robert Frost.
13. My favorite Robert McCloskey story about Homer Price is "mystery yarn."
14. The audience joined in when we sang "this land is your land."
15. We have read "the raven" and "annabel lee," two poems by Edgar Allan Poe.
16. In less than six seconds, Sean can recite "the duck."
17. My article, "teachers talk television," will be in this week's paper!
18. Our principal said we looked sleepy, so she sang "i'm a little teapot."
19. She started rock collecting after she read "volcanoes and gemstones!"
20. Let's talk about the story "what do fish have to do with anything?"

Chapter 12: Punctuation, pp. 105–110

Commas, pp. 105–106

Exercise A

1. I read three chapters, turned out the light, and fell asleep.
2. Do you want a green, red, or purple gel pen?
3. Julia plays soccer, runs track, and takes piano lessons during the school year.
4. Your jacket must be in the car, in the house, or at school.
5. When I have a test, when I have a difficult assignment, or when I'm having trouble with one of my subjects, my dad helps me study.

Exercise B

6. Did you like the short, lively tune the band just played?
7. The clean, shiny chrome sparkled in the sunlight.
8. The small, brown, furry squirrel jumped from tree to tree.
9. What an intelligent, thoughtful speech he gave!
10. His wild, spiked hair wouldn't stay inside the baseball cap.

Commas and Semicolons with Compound Sentences, pp. 107–108

Exercise A

1. We wanted to walk all the way, but we forgot our sneakers.
2. Felicia shot the last basket, and she won the game for our team!
3. Terence is my best friend, but I don't always agree with him.
4. The boys played well in the semifinals, yet they did not win the championship.
5. I ironed my shirt, but it got wrinkled in the suitcase.
6. Did you want to ride with us to the soccer game, or did you want to meet us there?
7. I developed the pictures, but I didn't bring them with me.
8. The script wasn't well written, nor were the characters well developed.
9. I wanted to do well on the test, so I went to the review session after school.
10. Have you read the book, or did you see the movie?

Exercise B

11. My dad made me a bookshelf; I helped him.
12. Amy was on her skateboard; Luisa was on her bicycle.
13. I would come with you, but I should walk my dog right now.
14. Kim ate all of her lunch; I couldn't finish all of mine.
15. The bells rang at 1:23; everyone looked startled.
16. I wrote a letter to the editor, and my older sister checked my spelling and punctuation.
17. Dad's computer was making a strange noise; I thought it was broken.
18. There are eighteen windows in the house; eleven of them are downstairs.
19. We signed up for the race; our goal is to place in the top twenty.
20. My grandmother always cheers me up, but I don't see her often enough.

Colons, pp. 109–110

Exercise A

1. Have the following people turned in their assignments: Greg, Brenda, Isabel, and Carlton?
2. The varieties of trees we planted are as follows: live oak, crape myrtle, and elm.
3. You will need the following items on your first day at school: pencils, a ruler, notebook paper, an eraser, and a ballpoint pen.
4. C
5. The student council is holding elections for the following positions: president, vice-president, secretary, and treasurer.
6. There are three things you should remember: speak clearly, speak slowly, and tell the truth.

Developmental Language Skills Answer Key

7. C
8. There are three places you should start looking for clues for the scavenger hunt: the basement, the linen closet, and the attic.
9. Can you bring me the following cleaning products: furniture polish, tile cleaner, scouring powder, and carpet deodorizer?
10. C

Exercise B
11. She has to be at volleyball practice at 5:15 this afternoon.
12. Dear Mr. Wells:
13. Please set your alarm for 7:15 A.M., so you can be at school by 8:30.
14. Dear Officer Scott:
15. Did you say that band practice starts at 1:00 this afternoon?
16. Does the orchestra begin playing at 6:30 or 7:00?
17. Dear Sir or Madam:
18. Dear Mayor Garcia:
19. The bus will leave at 8:15 in the morning.
20. Dear Dr. Moore:

Chapter 13: Punctuation, pp. 111–118

Underlining (Italics) and Quotation Marks with Titles, pp. 111–112

Exercise A

1. We watched the movie <u>West Side Story</u> in class last week.
2. This painting by Magritte is called <u>The Human Condition</u>.
3. Have you ever read <u>Robinson Crusoe</u>?
4. The photographs in <u>National Geographic</u> are really beautiful.
5. Did you see the editorial in today's <u>Morning Advocate</u>?
6. My parents grew up watching a show called <u>Wild Kingdom</u>.
7. Mozart's comic opera <u>The Magic Flute</u> is funny!
8. Who titled this sculpture <u>The Seated Sakyamuni</u>?
9. President Kennedy's book <u>Profiles in Courage</u> won a Pulitzer Prize.
10. Which character in the movie <u>Toy Story</u> is bravest?

Exercise B

11. Washington Irving wrote the story "The Legend of Sleepy Hollow."
12. My little brother sang "Jingle Bells" for two hours last night!
13. Jenny can recite the poem "The Dragons are Singing Tonight" by Jack Prelutzky.
14. Can you play the song "Greensleeves" on the recorder?
15. The article called "How to Clean Your Room in Five Minutes" is very funny.

Exercise C

Answers will vary. Sample answers are given.

16. song — "How High the Moon"
17. book — *Summer of the Monkeys*
18. poem — "Southbound on the Freeway"
19. painting — *A Girl with a Kitten*
20. play — *Reindeer Soup*

Quotation Marks, pp. 113–114

Exercise A

1. "When did the bell ring?" asked Nick.
2. David said, "I have to be home at six o'clock."
3. Max shouted, "Look at those elephants!"
4. "I finished all my homework," said Ann.
5. Uncle Phil stopped the car and said, "Do you need a ride?"
6. "Is the door locked?" asked Angela.
7. "We can go to my house after school," said Rita.
8. "You remembered my birthday!" exclaimed Simon.
9. Sara asked, "What time is the party?"
10. "I will pick you up at seven o'clock," said Dad.

Exercise B

11. "I will help you with those problems," said Frank, "**i**f you remember to bring your book."
12. "**T**his problem is really hard," said Kristin, "but I'll get it right this time."
13. "When," asked Miguel, "**a**re the science projects due?"
14. Evan pointed and said, "**M**y project is on that table."
15. "**I**f you are hungry," said Nancy, "you can make a sandwich."

Apostrophes, pp. 115–116

Exercise A

1. men's
2. mother's
3. fox's
4. window's
5. babies'

EXERCISE B
6. everybody's
7. our *or* ours
8. no one's
9. their *or* theirs
10. your *or* yours

EXERCISE C
11. shouldn't
12. can't
13. I've
14. they're
15. who's

Parentheses, pp. 117–118
EXERCISE A
1. We had more rain last month (fourteen inches) than we had all last year.
2. Presidents Thomas Jefferson and John Adams died on the same day (July 4, 1826).
3. El Greco (1541–1614) was a famous Spanish painter.
4. I don't have my jacket (I think I left it at home), so I'm really cold!
5. Do you want to see the movie (I heard it's good) or play a game?
6. In 1877, Thomas Alva Edison showed his cylinder phonograph to the editors of *Scientific American* (a famous magazine).
7. The first woman in space (Valentina Tereshkova) traveled around the earth forty-five times.
8. One breed of horse grows to be only seventy-six centimeters (thirty inches) tall!
9. Hurry and get changed (we're leaving in five minutes) into your blue jumper.
10. Do you know a good skit (something silly) for us to perform at the assembly?

EXERCISE B
11. Harry Truman was President when World War II ended. (1884–1972)
12. We are going to the beach tomorrow. (after school)
13. Uncle Jack is arriving on Thursday. (he's my mother's brother)
14. The movie will come out in a few years. (2005, I think)
15. Don't tell Martin about the party! (it's a surprise party)
16. Add two cups of water to the pan. (sixteen ounces)
17. Who took her bright green pen? (or borrowed)
18. Christine's only sister runs track for her high school. (Marie)
19. Hurry and look at this odd-looking moth! (before it flies away)
20. Ms. Fenner said that it took her years to learn how to paint. (the art teacher)

Chapter 14: Spelling, pp. 119–130

Words with *ie* and *ei*, pp. 119–120

EXERCISE A
1. receipt
2. receive
3. foreign
4. believe
5. achieve
6. field
7. brief
8. conceive
9. sleigh
10. chief

EXERCISE B
11. niece
12. eight
13. reign
14. freight
15. forfeit
16. their
17. pieces
18. relieved
19. reindeer
20. height

Prefixes and Suffixes, pp. 121–122

EXERCISE A
1. precaution
2. misunderstand
3. undo
4. dislike
5. rewind

EXERCISE B
6. removal
7. politeness
8. lifelike
9. activity
10. tracing
11. pavement
12. hiking
13. lovely
14. careful
15. tasted

EXERCISE C
16. cheater
17. sleeping
18. dimmer
19. swimming
20. leaking

Plurals of Nouns, pp. 123–124

EXERCISE A
1. flashes
2. studios
3. birthdays
4. losses
5. pianos
6. boys
7. taxes
8. birches
9. bottles
10. cabinets

EXERCISE B
11. Chinese
12. pastries
13. women
14. trout *or* trouts
15. lobbies
16. geese
17. counties
18. salmon *or* salmons
19. men
20. blueberries

Words Often Confused A, pp. 125–126

EXERCISE A
1. altogether
2. brake
3. all together
4. break
5. all ready
6. altogether
7. brake

Developmental Language Skills Answer Key

8. already
9. all together
10. all ready

EXERCISE B
11. course
12. chose
13. cloths
14. choose
15. coarse

Words Often Confused B, pp. 127–128
EXERCISE A
1. It's
2. here
3. dessert
4. its
5. hear

EXERCISE B
6. passed
7. loose

8. past
9. led
10. lose

Words Often Confused C, pp. 129–130
EXERCISE A
1. their
2. They're
3. there
4. Their
5. piece

EXERCISE B
6. your
7. too
8. weak
9. Who's
10. You're

Chapter 15: Correcting Common Errors, pp. 131–132

Exercise A
Some answers may vary.

1. In September, class representatives ~~in the cafeteria~~ met and form**ed** committees.
2. Th**e**n, everyone chose ~~their~~ **his or her** job.
3. One group collect**ed** bags and boxes, and several asked ~~his or her~~ **their** parents to help with transportation.
4. During October, the journalism teacher ~~learned~~ **taught** us how to write press releases, and we ~~sended~~ **sent** the press releases to the newspapers and radio stations.
5. We s**a**t up an information booth in the hallway and ~~had~~ hung posters in the neighborhood.
6. Working with teachers, ~~maps were drew by one group~~ **one group drew maps**.
7. On a sunny Saturday morning, we all ~~meet~~ **met** in the parking lot and got ~~their~~ **our** assignments.
8. Parents ~~had~~ went with students to knock on doors and ~~except~~ **accept** donations of canned food.
9. Some neighbors had already ~~brung his~~ **brought their** donations to the school.
10. We could ~~of~~ **have** collected more, but there was~~n't~~ no more room in the boxes.

Exercise B
Some answers may vary.

11. An article in the <u>Morning News</u> said that the center will be open every day except m**M**onday.
12. According to the article in the N**n**ewspaper, the center will be named the l**L**illian c**C**arter y**Y**outh c**C**enter.
13. The reporter wrote**,** **"**Everyone agrees that m**M**rs. Carter**,** a well-known volunteer in the neighborhood**,** deserves the honor.**"**
14. After we skate**,** we can play volleyball**;** maybe we can watch a movie t**o**o.
15. Oops**!** I'd better get off the phone now**;** it**'**s ~~all ready~~ **already** time to leave for the ceremony**.**

Developmental Language Skills Answer Key

Chapter 16: Writing Effective Sentences, pp. 133–42

Complete Sentences and Sentence Fragments, pp. 133–34

Exercise A

1. F
2. S
3. F
4. S
5. F
6. S
7. S
8. F
9. F
10. S

Exercise B

Answers will vary.

11. Sarah is a new friend of mine.
12. Mary went to her cousin's house.
13. Dad turned off the stove.
14. Jessica is still in the classroom.
15. Ask Mr. Peterson about the meeting after school.

Run-on Sentences, pp. 135–36

Exercise A

1. Please take me to the store. My science project is due tomorrow.
2. Do you have red and blue markers? I need a display board, too.
3. My project is about magnets. What topic did you pick?
4. Maybe I will win a prize. Last year my project won second place.
5. My report is finished. I still need to make a graph and a chart.

Exercise B

6. Finish your homework first, and then you can call Michael.
7. I want to buy those shoes, but I don't have enough money.
8. Did Karen borrow my book, or did Jeff borrow it?
9. My brother wants a dog, but we don't have a fenced yard.
10. My grandparents built this house in 1960, and they lived in it for almost forty years.

Combining Sentences by Inserting Words, pp. 137–38

Exercise A

1. Is your book report due tomorrow?
2. The gentle rain fell on the flowers.
3. Leonardo da Vinci was a famous Italian artist and scientist.
4. Her blue coat was torn on a nail.
5. The stars are shining brightly tonight.

Exercise B

6. The dog is snoring loudly again.
7. His joyful song filled the air.
8. She knocked softly on the door.
9. The cook poured the batter into the oiled pan.
10. She is a nationally famous track star.

Combining Sentences by Inserting Groups of Words, pp. 139–40

Exercise A

Answers may vary slightly.

1. The electricity went out in the middle of the night.
2. Determined to win the music award, Bill practiced every day.
3. The rooster, crowing at dawn, woke us all up.
4. I waited for the bus for more than an hour.
5. Terrified of the dog, the little boy started to cry.

EXERCISE B

6. My mother, the oldest of five sisters, comes from a big family.
7. The new building, our town's library, was painted bright blue and green.
8. Sara, my younger sister, is the tallest person in my family.
9. Jeanne, a new student in our class, just moved here from France.
10. Kevin wrote a letter to his aunt Ann, a major in the army.

Combining Sentences by Using Connecting Words; Joining Subjects and Verbs, pp. 141–42

EXERCISE A

1. The bird dove into the water and caught a fish.
2. Matt or Sandy will bring the refreshments.
3. The boy sat on the ground and looked up at the tree.
4. I tripped but did not fall.
5. He wrapped and taped the package.

EXERCISE B

6. My body is tired, but my mind is wide awake.
7. Come over when you get home from school, or call me on the telephone.
8. The audience clapped loudly, and the musicians took another bow.
9. I would lend you some paper, but I don't have any.
10. The band began to play, and both teams ran onto the field.

Developmental Language Skills Answer Key